Book 2

learn to play the french horn!

A carefully graded method
that emphasizes good tone production,
builds a sound rhythmic sense and
develops well-rounded musicianship.

by William Eisenhauer

WARMING-UP

One of the most important parts of the horn player's routine is a good warm-up. Before playing any exercise or ensemble piece, you should spend some time on long tones, lip slurs and tonguing. Warm-up time varies with every player, so you will have to experiment a bit. The warm-ups given on the following pages are not meant to be played all at once. Choose some from each category so as to make a well-rounded routine.

*In this pattern use ½ fingering throughout.

TONGUING WARM-UPS

Play each exercise at various speeds. Try to develop a light and bouncing staccato. Take deep breaths to support your tone. Use a small tongue motion.

Numbers 2-6 above should be played using the following variations of articulation:

A REVIEW OF SIXTEENTHS

Write in arrows to show where each beat falls.

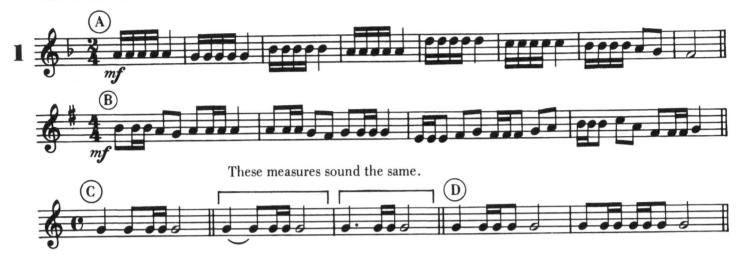

These measures sound the same.

WILLIAM TELL

ROSSINI

CHROMATIC FINGER BUSTER

Andante at first
Allegro when notes are secure

THEME (from Mendelssohn's "Italian Symphony" No. 4)

1 Andante con moto *(with motion)*

STACCATO ETUDE

2 Moderato

Reviewing the ♩.♪ rhythm

MARYLAND, MY MARYLAND

3 Moderato

COMPARING DOTTED RHYTHMS

4 Ⓐ Ⓑ

LIP BUILDER

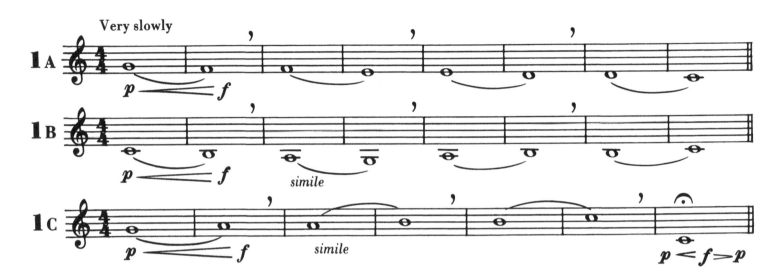

RHYTHMIC PUZZLER IN 2/4

THE GIFT TO BE SIMPLE (Duet)

SHAKER FOLK SONG

A REVIEW OF $\frac{6}{8}$ TIME

Allegro (in 2)

1

WHEN JOHNNY COMES MARCHING HOME

Allegretto

2

EXERCISE IN INTERVALS

Andante (in 6)

3

MELODY IN F

Allegretto

4

$\frac{3}{8}$ TIME

Compare the two versions of a portion of "America." They should sound the same. Be careful when you estimate speed; make sure that you know the unit of beat.

IN THE STYLE OF BEETHOVEN

TUNE IN $\frac{3}{8}$

W.E.

POSTHORN FANFARE (Duet)

* *molto* means much. *Molto rit.* means a large ritard.

NEW DYNAMICS

pp = pianissimo — very soft

ff = fortissimo — very loud

These markings are seen frequently in compositions and arrangements. Remember that dynamics are *relative* terms. Never spoil the beauty of a tone by playing too loudly or too softly.

GAVOTTE

TELEMANN

SKILL BUILDER

BARBARA ALLEN

TRADITIONAL

LYRIC PIECES

A beautiful legato style is essential in learning to play the french horn. Good tone quality, true pitch and sensitive phrasing are all necessary to developing a style. In the legato, songlike pieces that follow, strive for a singing tone quality. Listen to your own playing very critically. How can it be improved?

LULLABYE

BRAHMS

COME THOU, ALMIGHTY KING

DRINK TO ME ONLY WITH THINE EYES

TRADITIONAL

* Poco = little; poco rit. = a little ritard.

NEW NOTE — Low F — 1(0)

Form your mouth as though saying TAH ⟶ F — Slur on the repeat.

1

THE F MAJOR SCALE (2 Octaves)

2

COME DANCE (A Rhythmic Puzzler)

Allegro, with spirit

CZECH FOLK TUNE

3

THEME FROM SYMPHONY NO. 1 (Duet)

Allegro non troppo*

BRAHMS

4

* means Allegro but not too fast.

(*sfz* = Sforzando—an emphasis on a note)

There are many notes on the french horn that have more than one fingering. Sometimes these *alternate fingerings* are used to make a passage easier to play. In this exercise, and others like it that follow, they are used so that the entire passage may be played with the same fingering and so that LIP SLURS can be practiced.

SYNCOPATION STUDIES

Notice that 2A and 2B sound exactly the same.

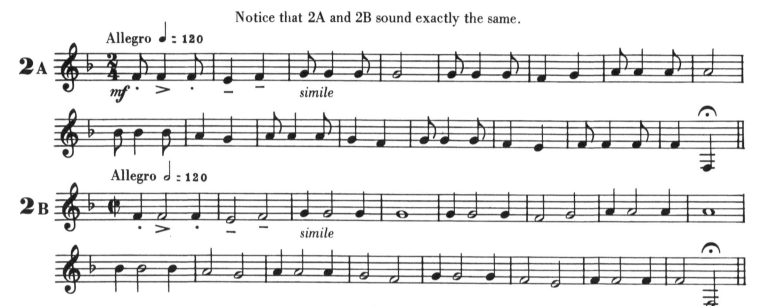

HAVA NAGILA

ISRAELI FOLK TUNE

I AM THE VERY MODEL OF A MODERN MAJOR GENERAL
from "The Pirates of Penzance"

Allegro, leggiero *

GILBERT AND SULLIVAN

ETUDE, Op. 10, No. 3

Andante, flexibly

CHOPIN

LA RASPA (Duet)

Allegro (in 2)

MEXICAN FOLK SONG

*Leggiero=lightly.

D.C. al fine

13

THE KEY OF Eb MAJOR

New key signature.
(B, E and A are all flat.)

Eb ARPEGGIO

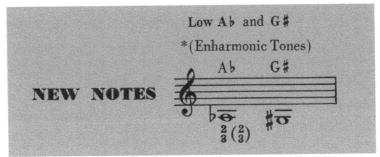

NEW NOTES

Low Ab and G#

*(Enharmonic Tones)

Ab   G#

Eb SKILL BUILDERS

Tongue the 1st time; slur on the repeats.

THE RAKES OF MALLOW

IRISH FOLK TUNE

Moderato

Change octaves on repeat.

simile

*Enharmonic: Tones which have same pitch and the same fingerings but a different letter name.

14

PROCESSIONAL MARCH (from the "Emperor" String Quartet)
(Duet)

HAYDN

Andantino

SKILL BUILDERS WITH SCALES AND ARPEGGIOS

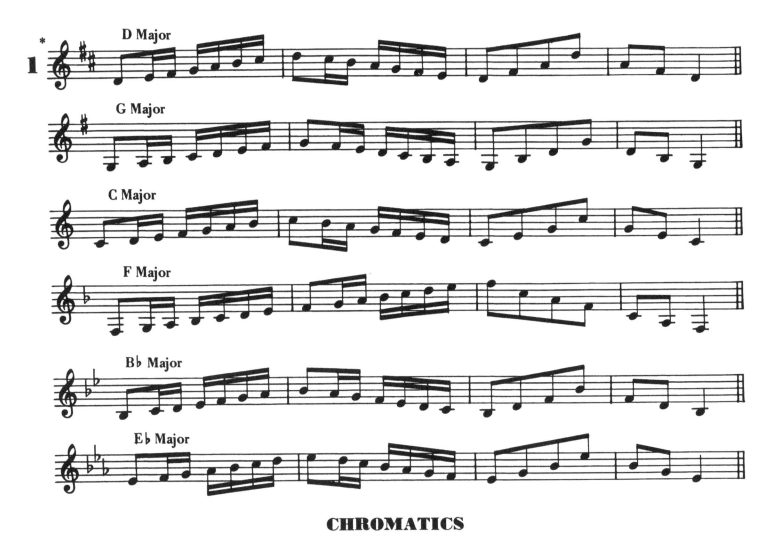

CHROMATICS

A CHROMATIC SCALE is one which is constructed only of half steps. A chromatic scale can be written starting on any tone. It is usually written with sharps when ascending and flats when descending.

Play tongued and slurred.

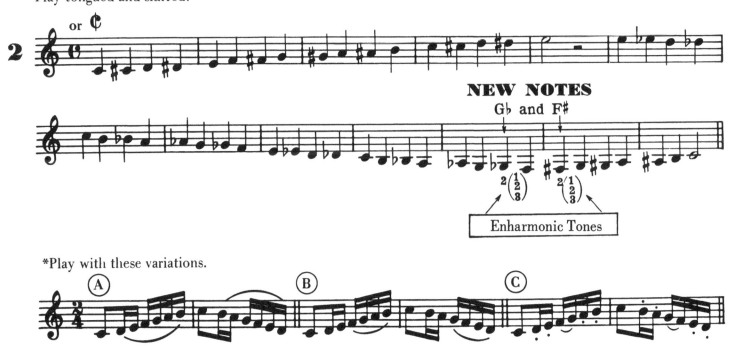

*Play with these variations.

WARM-UPS (with Alternate Fingerings)

TRIPLETS

TRIUMPHAL MARCH (from "Aida")

VERDI

SAILING, SAILING (Duet)

A NEW SYNCOPATION

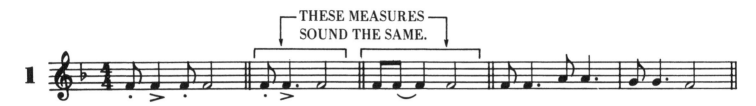

HE'S GOT THE WHOLE WORLD IN HIS HANDS

REST MEASURES

When playing in a band or orchestra, you will probably have some measures in which you do not play. These MEASURES REST must be counted so that you can play your part at the right time.

A prolonged rest may be written in your part like this:

Both of these mean that you have three measures to count that contains no music for you. The correct way to do this is to THINK or COUNT SILENTLY "1-2-3-4-;2-2-3-4-;3-2-3-4-". Notice that the first count in each measure is the number of the measure. Don't forget to count ONLY the number of beats in each measure as determined by the meter signature!

*Rall. (rallentando) = gradually slower.

STUDIES IN STYLE

Be very careful to make your articulation fit the style of music that you are playing. In the following examples make the difference between legato and staccato very clear.

1 Allegretto

TWO SELECTIONS FOR CONTRAST

MARCH "FORWARD"

CHARLES GOUSE

2 March tempo ♩. = 120

HOME ON THE RANGE

3 Moderato (in 6)

ETUDE FOR CONTRASTS

W.E.

NOW IS THE MONTH OF MAYING
(Duet)

T. MORLEY

THE KEY OF A MAJOR

A MAJOR FINGER BUSTER

PRAYER from "Hansel and Gretel"

E. HUMPERDINCK

*Poco a poco = little by little ; poco a poco cresc. = gradually louder and louder.

STUDIES IN STACCATO

A light, rapid staccato is one of the horn player's best tools. Use only the tip of your tongue. Look at yourself in a mirror as you play. Make sure that your throat is relaxed. If you see any movement in your throat or the lower jaw, review your method of tonguing so that bad habits are not formed.

Make sure that your third valve finger remains on the valve button. Don't let it curl under.

THE SECRET

L. GAUTIER

ENDURANCE

A major problem for any brass instrument is endurance. Lip slurs, legato songs and articulation studies are all important in developing endurance. Rest for several minutes after playing No. 1 as a warmup.

CORONATION MARCH

MEYERBEER

WE HAVE BUILT A STATELY MANSION
(from "Academic Festival Overture")
(Trio)

BRAHMS

Much music is written in one meter throughout. There are, however, many beautiful compositions that change meter. In the examples below, the quarter notes will be of equal speed.

SHENANDOAH

AMERICAN SEA CHANTY

LOWLANDS

SCOTCH

SKILL BUILDERS

ETUDE IN A

CHORALE ST. ANTHONY
(Trio)

This may be used as a duet by playing the 1st and 2nd parts only.

Andante

NEW NOTES

1
G Major Scale

LIP BUILDERS

Support your tone with plenty of air. Connect each tone smoothly and use only the fingering given.

2

CHROMATIC SKILL BUILDERS

(F#)

3

Practice tonguing also.

ETUDE IN

ARBAN

Moderato

4

OH SUSANNA

Allegro

5

Change octaves on repeat.

FURIANT

SLAVONIC DANCE

RHYTHMIC PUZZLER IN $\frac{6}{8}$

PRESTO POLKA (Duet)

DUET IN $\frac{3}{8}$ TIME

Allegretto

NIEMANN

LARGE SKIPS IN LEGATO

In the following LIP BUILDERS you will find that lip slurs are required that have larger intervals than found in previous exercises. A helpful technique is to hear the higher note BEFORE you play it. At the precise moment that you want the note to change, arch the back of your tongue upward as if saying EEEE. Make sure that you blow a STEADY stream of air. There should be no pause between notes.

LYRIC PIECE

ON WINGS OF SONG

MINOR SCALES

A MINOR SCALE has a different sequence of half and whole steps than does the major scale. There are three forms of MINOR SCALE, the NATURAL FORM, the HARMONIC FORM and the MELODIC FORM. Study and play the following examples. Listen to them carefully. Discuss with your teacher the differences between MAJOR and MINOR.

ETUDE IN G MINOR

W.E.

WALTZ IN A MINOR

CHARLES GOUSE

Comparing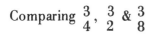

A, B & C sound the same

COME THOU, ALMIGHTY KING

COVENTRY CAROL (Trio)

* Sostenuto = sustained; held to the fullest value.

LIP BUILDERS

Support your tone with plenty of air.

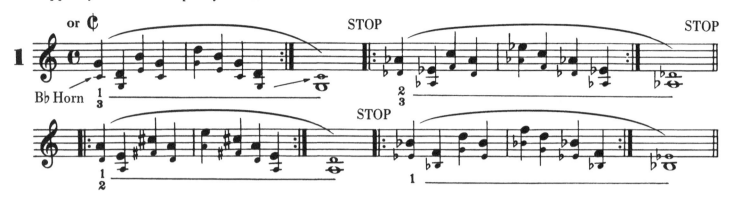

A RHYTHMIC MYSTERY

HIGH NOTE TUNE

CAPRICCIO ITALIEN (Duet)

TSCHAIKOWSKY

TWO SOLOS FOR EXPRESSION

IRISH BALLAD

LONDONDERRY AIR

LIP BUILDERS

Remember to use only the fingerings given and use sufficient air to support your tone.

GIGUE (Duet)

Allegretto

BOISMORTIER

(rit. 2nd time)

LOLLY TOO-DUM

Animato = lively
Subito = suddenly

GOD OF OUR FATHERS
(Trio)

*Maestoso = majestically.

TONGUING STUDY

1

Practice both octaves.

SKILL BUILDERS

2 Allegro, leggiero

mf

3

RIGADOON (from "Suite No. 5")

PURCELL

4

Fine

f

D.C. al Fine

mp

SOME PROBLEMS IN TIES
(Rhythmic Puzzlers)

Is this Major or Minor?

CIELITO LINDO

Moderato, leggiero

AIDA

Moderato

VERDI

THE KEY OF E MAJOR

SKILL BUILDER IN E

JEANIE WITH THE LIGHT BROWN HAIR

S. FOSTER

MARCHING TO PRETORIA
(Duet)

When any of the triple meters; 3/4, 3/8 or 3/2 are played at a fast tempo, it may be inconvenient to count each beat. When speed is essential, each measure should receive *one* beat.

MERRY WIDOW WALTZ

F. LEHAR

SWEET BETSY FROM PIKE

LIP BUILDER

REVIEWING THE FLAT KEYS

THEME FROM THE FIFTH SYMPHONY

Andantino   TSCHAIKOWSKY (adapted)

HAIL TO THE CHIEF

March tempo

ON WINGS OF SONG (Again)

This song may be played either
in a moderate 6 or slow 2.

MENDELSSOHN

NEW NOTES

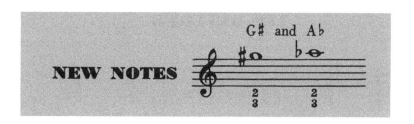

G# and Ab

THE KEY OF Ab MAJOR

New Signature:

Practice both octaves.

Ab

1

2

ETUDE IN Ab

W.E.

3

Practice also in A.

When practicing in A, sharp these notes:

CANON FOR TWO

A canon is a composition in which one voice imitates another.
The combination of these two parts creates harmony.

Andante

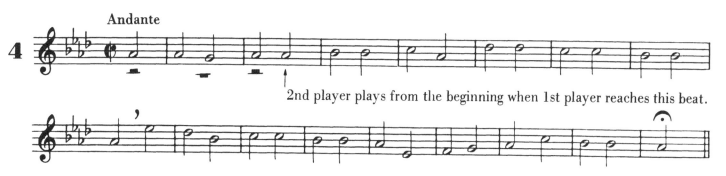

4

2nd player plays from the beginning when 1st player reaches this beat.

LIP BUILDER

1

THE ASH GROVE

2 Moderato *mf* *cresc.* Fine D.C. al fine *f*

$\frac{9}{8}$ TIME (Compound meter)

3

1 2 3 4 5 6 7 8 9   1 2 3 4 5 6 7 8 9
1 & a 2 & a 3 & a   1 & a 2 & a 3 & a

PILGRIM'S CHORUS (from "Tannhauser")

WAGNER

4 Andante

Play also in A. *mf* tenuto

mp

mf

f rit.

cresc.

ff

NEW NOTE — High A

EXTENDING THE KEY OF A MAJOR

BEAUTIFUL DREAMER

STEPHEN FOSTER

$\frac{12}{8}$ TIME (Compound meter)

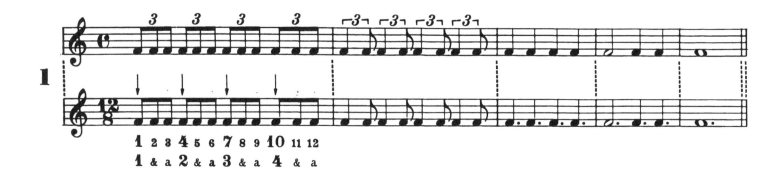

SOLDIERS CHORUS (from "Faust")

GOUNOD

ROUND FOR FOUR HUNTERS*

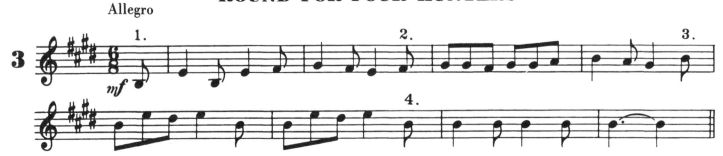

*This round may be played by 2, 3, or 4 players.

THE LAST OF THE LIP BUILDERS

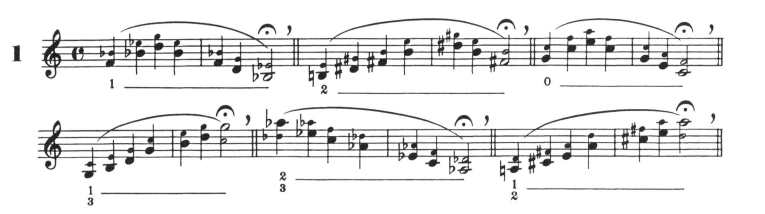

FUGUE*

*A "fugue" is a composition in which voices imitate one another as in a round. However, the fugue has sections where the voices do not imitate one another *exactly* as they do in a round. A fugue may be written for two to five players.

MAJOR SCALES AND ARPEGGIOS

FINGERING CHART

The fingerings for the B♭ horn are shown in parenthesis.

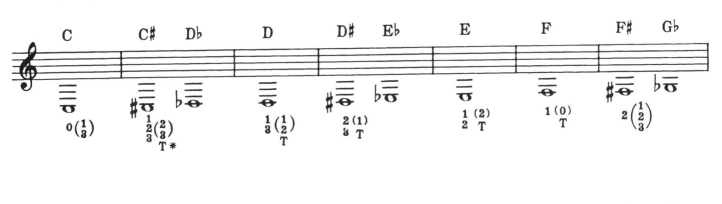

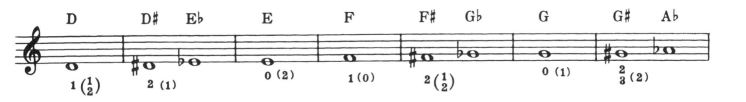

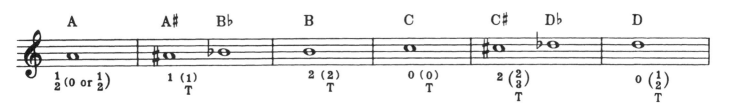

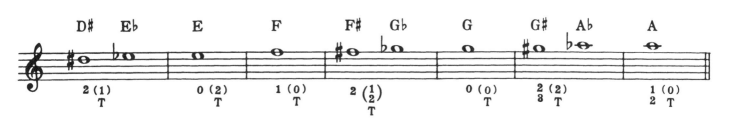

*When playing the double (F-B♭) horn, the B♭ fingering is accomplished by pressing the thumb valve (T). In this chart the letter T appears only under those B♭ fingerings that are most suitable for the double horn. Opinion differs as to the changeover from F to B♭ therefore follow your teacher's instructions.

A Small Dictionary of Musical Terms

SPEED

Accelerando (accel.) . . . . Speeding up
Adagio . . . . Slow and deliberate
Allegretto . . . . A bit slower than allegro
Allegro . . . . Lively and fast
Andante . . . . "Walking speed" . . . . . comfortable
Andantino . . . . A little faster than andante
Grave . . . . Slow, serious
Larghetto . . . . A little faster than Largo
Largo . . . . Slow, broad and solemn
Moderato . . . . A moderate speed
Prestissimo . . . . As fast as you can play
Presto . . . . Very fast
Vivace . . . . Brisk . . . fast
Remember that all tempo markings are *relative*

DYNAMICS

cresc. or ⎯⎯⎯⎯⎯ . . . . *crescendo* . . . . getting gradually stronger (louder)
decresc. or ⎯⎯⎯⎯ or dim. . *decrescendo* or *diminuendo* . . . . getting gradually weaker (softer)
sf or sfz . . . . *sforzando* . . . . . with sudden emphasis
ff . . . . *fortissimo* . . . . . very strong
f . . . . *forte* . . . . . strong
mf . . . . *mezzo-forte* . . . . moderately strong
mp . . . . *mezzo-piano* . . . . moderately soft
p . . . . *piano* . . . . . softly
pp . . . . *pianissimo* . . . . . very quietly

STYLE

Accel. *accelerando* . . . to speed up gradually
A tempo . . . . in the original speed
Dolce . . . . sweetly
Legato . . . . smoothly, connected
Leggiero . . . . lightly
Maestoso . . . . majestically
Poco . . . . little
Poco a poco . . . . little by little
Rit. . . . . *ritard* . . . to slow down gradually
Simile . . . . the same as before
Sostenuto . . . . sustained
Staccato . . . . separated
Tenuto . . . . held out to full value